Messy THRiLLing Life

Also by
Sabrina Ward Harrison

Spilling Open

Brave on the Rocks

Messy THRilling Life

Life

The ART of Figuring out how to Live

SaBRINA Ward Harrison

FOREWORD
By
LAURIE
WAGNER

Villard

FOREWORD

I lay in bed one morning at five o'clock, searching for an order. Lay there after my husband had gotten up for his shower, lay there after my eight-year-old daughter had climbed in beside me, lay there nudging our dog to move over, lay there listening to the dreamy murmurings of another daughter in the next room. I had stumbled across a line the day before, and I was repeating it to myself. "You make your plans. You make your plans," I echoed in the dark, hoping the next word would follow, and the word after that, until I had found my order and could build the foreword to Sabrina's book, word by word. And if not a real foreword, then at least a path that would lead me to the place where the rest of the foreword would be revealed. After a few moments more words floated my way: "And then a great wind comes along. You make your plans and then a great wind comes along." I liked the line because it reminded me of being in Sabrina's Berkeley studio some months ago when she invited me, friend and fellow writer, to help her put her own words in order.

I wish you could have seen the studio wall and all the paper, sheets and sheets of paper and a few napkins with scribbles tacked to the wall in long vertical rows. A wall so tall you needed to stand on a ladder to tack the writings up high enough because there was so much.

We were making a story. Sabrina's story. The stories in this book.

She'd found a beginning, the place where she felt her year of writing had begun, and there was a piece after that, and one after that, all running down the rows. It was a visual map of Sabrina's life in the last year, a way to bring to life the literal and emotional journey she had taken. There was a move to New York. There was art. Self-discovery. A pair of fancy pink sequined shoes. There were taxis and tears, bartenders and being alone. There was a man. Each poem and journal entry was a stepping-stone from one moment to the next.

Sometimes Sabrina sat back on a little stool, head cocked and gazing dizzily at the wall as I squinted at the writing. "How about this one here?" I'd say, moving pages from one end of the wall to another part entirely. Then Sabrina would get up and rummage through a pile of yesterday's writing, saying, "Would this work?" Then I'd walk to the end of the wall, pick a piece, and say, "Let's move this one up."

Up and down, back and forth, climbing the little ladder, taking pieces at the end and moving them to the front, taking pieces in the middle out of the book forever, and Sabrina asking herself again and again, What is my journey about? What am I trying to say? Working together was magical. Intuitive. There was no formula, no right order to the story, no one way to tell it. We were two women dancing with a wall and looking for a way in. Any of the pieces could have begun the book.

It took us three days and much coffee to put all of Sabrina's writing in order. When we felt something was missing,

Sabrina would turn to a pile of photographs that she'd printed the day before—images of rooftops, portraits of people—and she'd begin to write. In the end we stood back from the wall, satisfied and even a little smug, with the neat little path that we'd laid.

Many people leave their windows open in California, even on chilly spring days, as Sabrina did when we left the studio that day. And there must have been quite a flurry, because when she came back she saw all of her writing, not on the wall where we had carefully placed it, but on the floor in a swooshy-wooshy mess. It was a tangle of tales. A terrible tribute to our toiling.

You make your plans and then a great wind comes along.

And so Sabrina did the only thing one can do, in life and in the studio. She picked up the pages and began again. You make your plans and then a great wind comes along and you begin again.

We didn't remember which piece came first. We hadn't numbered the pages. We started over. Got more coffee, put music on, and Sabrina said, "You know, I'm thinking we could start with this piece," and in a day she'd created a different book entirely.

And I tell you this story, want to show you the swooshy-wooshy mess on the floor, because it reminds me of how life really is. How we make our plans and how tempting it is to believe that if we can just find the right order to our words, our stories, if we can find the right order to our lives, the right relationship, the right body, the family, the career, if we can just put these elements into place, then . . . then . . .

Then there's that wind again.

This is not a story about foiled plans and what's the use of trying anyway. This is precisely a story about making things: making stories, making plans, lists, and making love in the face of the inevitable messiness we will encounter; in the face of the great wind which will carry us to its own unquestionable destination. The entries in this book are about plans made and plans broken. They are poems and musings about love and loss and how a young woman navigates her way with words, images, and color through the turbulent and complex world around her. And in the end, it turns out that maybe it's not the order of our words and our stories that's so important, but how we pick them up off of the floor and how we hold them, how we live them and how we begin again.

Welcome to the thrilling and colorful world of Sabrina Ward Harrison, girl extraordinaire and master mess maker.

LAURIE WAGNER

This BOOK is dedicated
to my sister,
Anna
with so much love

Remember building the best fort ever? And then how the dog charged through the living room and across the pillows and how the blanket slid out from the stack of books holding it down, and how the whole thing fell apart, but also how this broken down mess was what got you outside, out to that wide field where you found some jacked-up old wood and a random shoe, and then how you found yourself starting again, building something altogether new. How you sat there with dirt under your finger nails, digging away, and how the sun was setting and you looked up to see a new view emerging from across the wide field and over the lake. A world that was waiting for you, but which you wouldn't have seen if the dog hadn't charged through the living room → that's how these pages are made. They are bits and beginnings, little forts I set up in my studio and in my dreams. They're the beginnings of conversations to be continued. They are notes to myself, all the things I want to remember — A winter night spent dancing on my rooftop feeling my life was complete as is; I was right where I was meant to be in the world. This book captures the way I carry these moments that make up my life, the way my questions look to me and the way I find what is true for my life.

This book is not a straight line, with all the perfect pieces filled in just right. This is a document of how we can traipse about wondering, how we can devise plans and theories on how to make life feel better, more safe and right more beautiful, and how all the while our life, this big messy thrilling LIFE, is waiting for us to step into, to dance to, to write about and to live. This is a book about doing just that — Sabrina

June 10 2004

WHAT I found THERE

Admitting
~~Today~~

WANT
~~CRAVE~~
~~should~~
~~CHANGE~~
SURRENDER
Release
HOPE
~~need~~
Be
ARE

Become

WAnt

HOLd
hold

HOLD

EMBARRASSED
ASHAMED

Hidden

secret
chOICE
FREEDOM

I AM A WOMAN WHO WANTs tO
ONLy weigh 123 POUNDs and
sometimes thinks
I am A WOMAN that could Be tHE ANSWER
who likes Her
STOMACH flat and wants
TO seem like it Doesn't
MATTER all that Much
I AM A WOMAN
who wants
TO MAKE POWERFul
ART of tHis WORLD
I am A woman
who can feel
so lonely
At the most
unexpected
TIMes
AND sometimes
I can't ask
DIRECTLY
or tell you
HOW upset
I really feel
AND I hope
I'll grow out
OF it.
I AM A WOMAN who
sometimes forgets about
POetry and reading in
tHE SHADe.

GIRLS SEEM VERY LEGGY IN THIS CITY.

THEIR legs
GO ON AND
ON

WHERE DID they
All come from?
WHATs going on?

SEX
MONEY
POWER
SCANDAL
HAMISH
GOTHAM

5'4½
SAB

A less k.
Drew
these

VOGUE DESIGN

I dlit
I Must SAy,
It's A Bit
MucH.

I'm 5'4½ w 1

PATTERN PATRON
A   C   E   B

I want to leave
a Dance.
I want to
Let it rip
I want to
FIND NEW
rooms
inside
myself
I don't
want to
write myself
off as weak.
I want
to
strengthen
EVERYTHING
HEART
Much
Lilli
NICOLE

W. 10th
WEEHAWKE
sarabeth
love getting there as much as being there.
I DIDn't really think it would feel this way at this age
west side highway

I AM A WOMAN V.

WHO WANTS TO START fresh
and most of the Time
I feel small
WHEN I TAKE
My Boots off

I AM A WOMAN

I AM A WOMAN
WHO needs
HER OWN
ROLE Models
And doesn't want
TO Be one for
anyone else
Maybe one
that
speaks up
FOR THE
Mixed Bag
OF HUMAN

Whoever compares HER Body TO

I AM and silently wishes

introductions.

SHE DIDN'T anymore.

OTHER WOMEN'S

SIZE 8

PATTERN/PATRON

Very Easy
Vogue
Patterns

$3.00
$3.30 IN CANADA

Being a Bold
soft
sorely
Brave
Woman

A
Finding
Misplacing
copying

takes A lot of keys.

losing my keys.

and I want to be loved, but not changed to fit them.
I want to live louder but not feel like a selfish person for doing so.

I want to go crazy

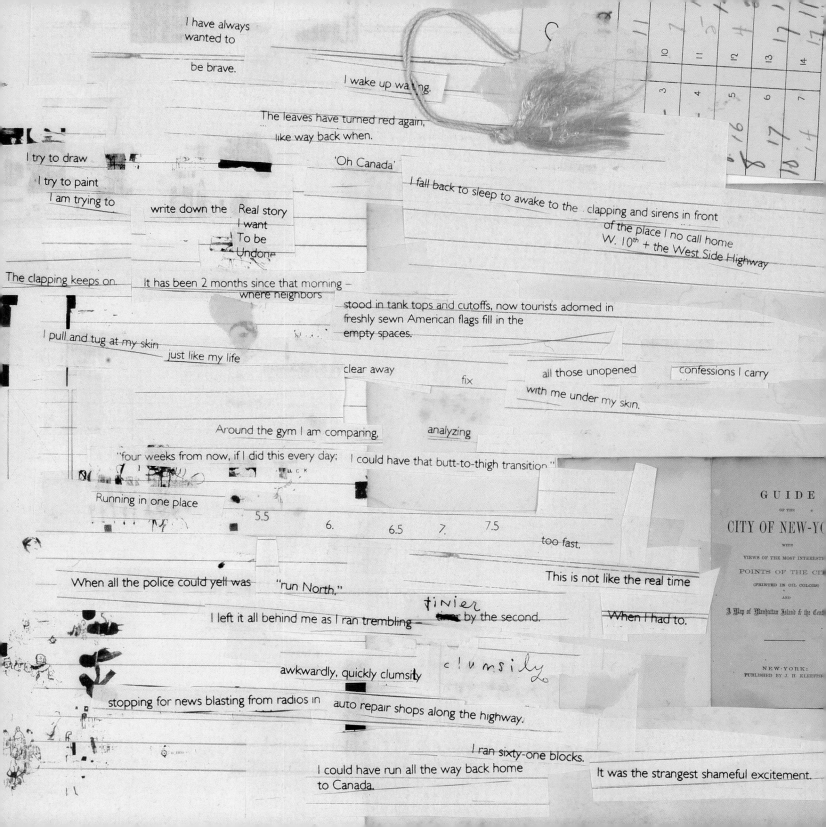

I have always
wanted to

be brave.

I wake up waiting.

The leaves have turned red again,
like way back when.

I try to draw

'Oh Canada'

I try to paint

I fall back to sleep to awake to the   clapping and sirens in front

I am trying to

write down the   Real story
I want
To be
Undone

of the place I no call home
W. 10th + the West Side Highway

The clapping keeps on.   It has been 2 months since that morning –
where neighbors

stood in tank tops and cutoffs, now tourists adorned in
freshly sewn American flags fill in the
empty spaces.

I pull and tug at my skin

just like my life

clear away   fix   all those unopened   confessions I carry

with me under my skin.

Around the gym I am comparing,   analyzing

"four weeks from now, if I did this every day;   I could have that butt-to-thigh transition"

Running in one place

5.5   6.   6.5   7.   7.5

too fast.

This is not like the real time

When all the police could yell was   "run North."

tinier
by the second.

When I had to.

I left it all behind me as I ran trembling –

awkwardly, quickly clumsily   clumsily

stopping for news blasting from radios in   auto repair shops along the highway.

I ran sixty-one blocks.

I could have run all the way back home
to Canada.

It was the strangest shameful excitement.

GUIDE
OF THE
CITY OF NEW-YO
WITH
VIEWS OF THE MOST INTEREST
POINTS OF THE CI
(PRINTED IN OIL COLORS)
AND
A Map of Manhattan Island & the Cent

NEW-YORK:
PUBLISHED BY J. H. KLEEFISH

FRAGILE

UP

Back at the gym

I feel guilty I care about my

butt-to-thigh transition
In times like these.

Betting control?
Fit me in.

Size 12-13

Size 10-12

Smaller?

Stronger?

Size 8-9

Size 7-8

Size 6-7

The smaller you are the

better you'll fit?

Fit in?

Size 5-6

Size 4-5

Size 3-4

Fit him?

Size 1-2

I walk by the dry cleaners   on my way home

picking up the hemmed up jeans I got

at rags-a-go-go   on   W. 14th   I'll wear them to the park

with him this weekend

as if I always had

Next door there is a sale in body suits.

The windows are filled with ads for European gas masks

Winter is coming

It's time to get home

It's getting dark

I wonder if he ca

I gather up

Pack in tight

So I carry ON

this   old walk home

Thinking how long it has   been

since I was small

enough to lie down

in my mother's lap
and know

I didn't have to be afraid.

I feel a mixture of shy and powerful in this city. No one really knows me, and that feels free and a little scary

Start Here Again!

I miss Megan Brown
and the grand cards she
would send of
her life and her wisdom.
I miss her laugh with her great whites
and the wonderful bags she carries
and the late afternoon stable chores
and my MOM striding DOWN
to meet me, all Brown twinkle
gold light
and ruby
orange
lipstick
(she wears
everything
but PINK
and purple
I like that
in a gal.
I miss HORSES
MY MOM
I miss ALEX'S
bubbling
laughter
TODAY.

I went Back to the DARKROOM and
began printing again.
It feels like it has been years
surrendered my pride and asked for help.
                    setting up

and then the room
        was mine
    a little Darkroom in the
    middle of this whospery city

    QUIET.

printed Laurie's portrait first

    I love to watch

    the face appear
growing into the page
    Her face is RicH

all I wanted to write under the picture
was "I know How you feel"
            or "Me too"

    It's hard to give it up in THIs CITY
            Drop the sHowlders
            STOP clencHING

what will I   DO with the rest
of my
Life.

crabby
Annoying
Bitchy
lame
Pathetic
Mean
snarly
Needy
Plain
pushy
worn-out

PARTS of Me I really
don't like
when they
come out

we can't always be lovely + Glowing

I know I am always trying to come
from love,
and I don't all the time
I know I can be a pisser and
really annoying
I know I can burst into tears
at not the best times
I can listen
I can give

I can try my best
I know I can hurt people without
meaning to
I know I can love deeply
I grapple with all this stuff
don't we all?,
a bit

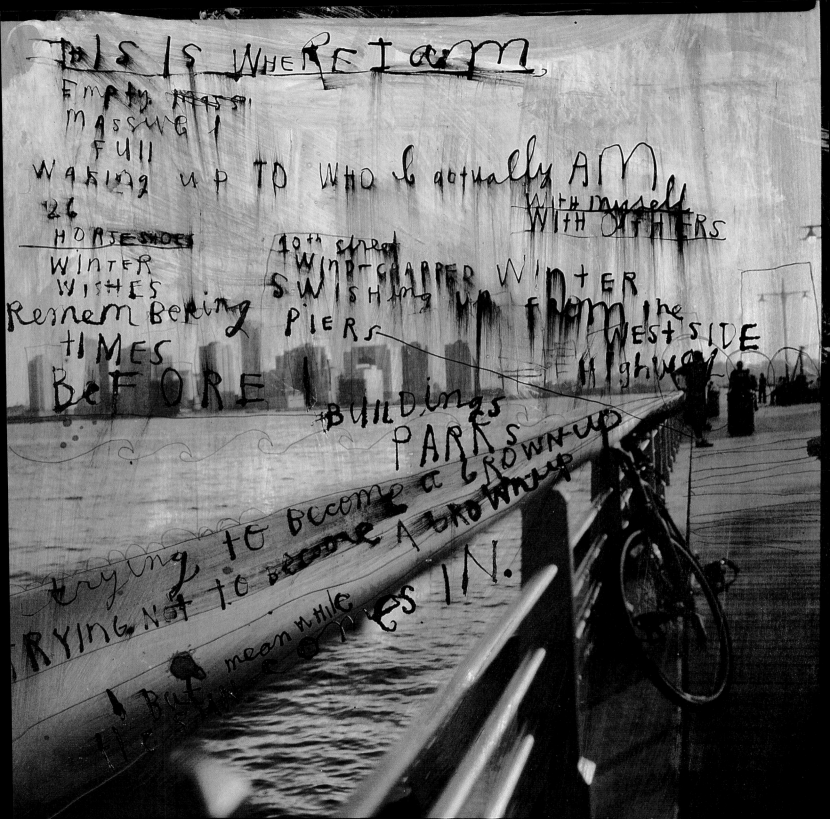

rolling forward in front of us as tangled as it gets.

TRAIN
1
9
falling out of LINE
ZOe
3
I WANT TO LEAVE
TRACES OF TRUTH.
TRACES OF WHAT
it actually feels LIKE
WHAT CAN BE TOLD TRUE
TODAY?
I APOLOGIZE SO OFTEN.
for myself.
I CATCH MYSELF
CAREfully
constructing
my actions to
"KEEP THE LOVE
STEADY"
THE ACCEPTANCE
STRONG.
THE UNDERSTANDING
in place.
I WANT TO GIVE IT
UP.
FALL OUT
OF LINE.
allow the way
it goes.

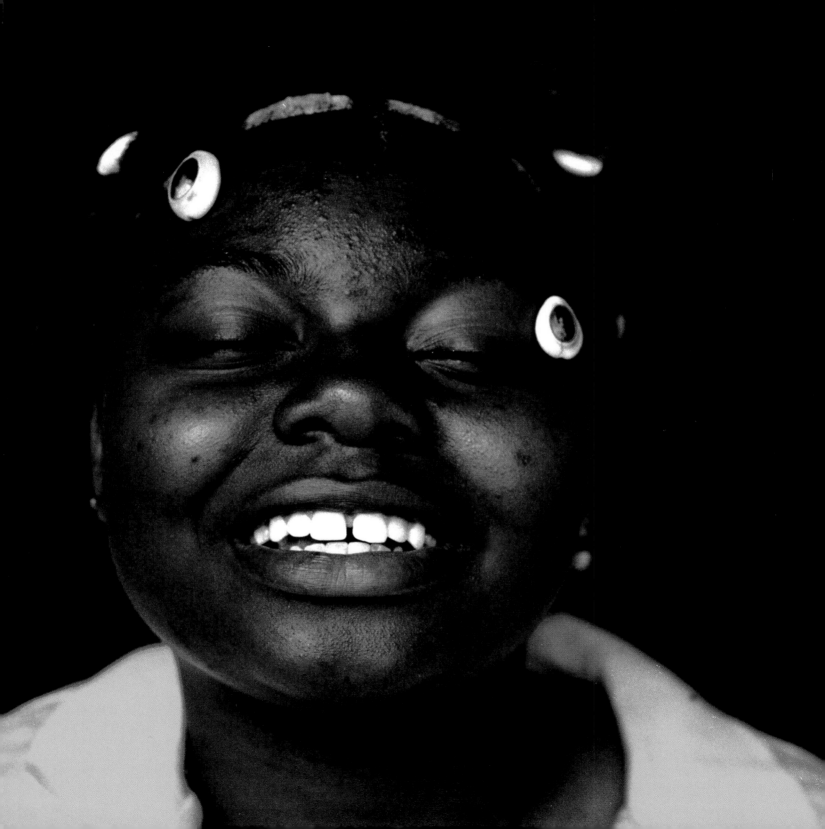

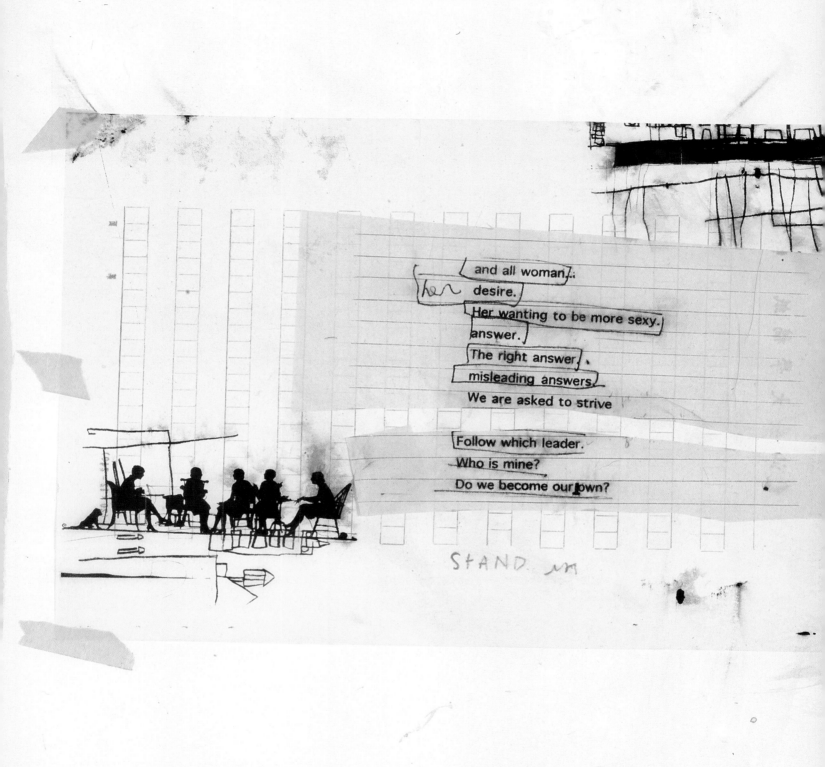

and all woman...
her desire.
Her wanting to be more sexy.
answer.
The right answer.
misleading answers
We are asked to strive

Follow which leader.
Who is mine?
Do we become our own?

STAND. m

GOING TO A BAR WITH
A GUY CAN really SUCK.
I HATE BEING CHECKED
OUT BY OTHER WOMEN. There
is supposed to BE ALL this
"sisterhood" but it seems
to fly out the WINDOW
it CAN BE SO FIERCE and
INTENSE. I try to remember
we are ALL JUST trying
TO MAKE OUR WAY
THROUGH. We ALL GET
NERVOUS and UNSURE
ABOUT OUR PLACE in
all THIS.

BUT IN THAT
BAR I FEEL
NAKED AND
ISOLATED SURROUNDED
BY A SWIRLING CROWD
OF smiles and spilling
ALCOHOL

AND I PLAY
along

HI BROWS

get

FORMATT* No. 5030

①WANDER in CENTRAL PARK
②WRITE, Write! Please write something DOWN
③ GO to ETHAN Hawke reading tonight
Be a simple FAN, DON't push FOR the COOL connection
EAT somefruit

SUN-SETTING SLUMP

- DUMB mood
- It's about Belonging
- Money worry
- Not writing DOWN ENOUGH detAILS
- Not making anything INTEResting
- WHERE DO I fit in NYC?
  - in the world?
  - inside me?

LEAVING ONLY Traces BEHIND US here

Isn't it overwelming SOMETIMES!? THIS _LIVING_ — tH is trying to Live MAKE IT HAPPEN, A full wide life or keep it HAPPENing then staying ON tHE BAll to keep on MAKIng your life LIFE WANts to slip by US WITH OUR TO-DO lists AND NEW YEAR'S RESOLUTIONS

LET ME DOWN

GRAYDOG cafe

7 th AVE

ONE WAY

the first
THIRTY-FOUR
things
on
my
Mind
today

Keep up

keep up

improve

more

better

faster

There is the gym and pilates, and a studio to pay for
and more and more paper
and ink piling up and

the memory of jenny read to hold
and Susan to visit

and an office
and a home to pick up   and sex to be had
that needs a system to keep it intact
and money to   keep making to keep it all "happening"

and paintings to be
making
and notes of landscapes and horses

and photos to   print and negatives to file
and jeans to fit into
and a city to move away from
and a new beginning all over again
and the bachelor to watch

and car insurance to get

YOGA
sleep   and medicine to refill   and a relationship to care for and old friends to write to
healthy food
and a sister to love
and 3 weddings to go to
and a future to plan
and a story to tell my grandparents   and cheaper cell phone service
and an ex-love to forget and a bookkeeper to find
a therapist to meet and horses to find
and printer ink to   refill

CENTRAL PARK like
the rest of THEM.
I Am a woman who
puts on her future when
SHE wakes up in his
ARMS and decisions
I AM A woman who
wants to FALL IN love
with her work the way
MEN DO. The way they
Put It FIRST AND
ME Second.

I AM Here to BE
DifFerent to BE
Full-Grown and
not girl and WOMAN
rattled WITH
QuEStIONS But A
WOMAN rEAdy t
MAKE NEW WORK
+ Find new ANSWErs
I AM A WOMAN WHO
DANcEd ON BARS WHO HAS

When I look at this photo I see darkness and pain, everything I was I was trying to avoid in New York that day. I had come to town to be on a big, national TV show for four minutes. I was there to talk about a book I had written and I had this notion that it would be a huge burst for my career, that in my four minutes I would shine so brightly, be so beautiful and brilliant that people would be coming up to me on the street saying, "I saw you on TV!" I imagined traipsing around the Village all day spending money I didn't have because I was so deserving and fascinatinating. But it was a bomb. The anchorwoman lost her place in the script and my four minutes of glory was chopped down to one and even then I lurched and stuttered and said things I didn't mean and then it was over and I found myself on the windy streets of New York feeling very used and very tired and very un-CBS-like.

I felt like I hadn't made the cut, that if I had been prettier or had had a little more coffee that morning, was smarter or more cool I would have been able to fix the anchor's mistake.

It was really hard for me to let it go.

When this picture was taken I was feeling like a nothing, , a reject.

Laurie Wagner

Here I sit and the rain comes down
again and it is nearing the end

of April and I am in

we will go,
and more will come
and be here after us,

on this   ground,

knowing more

from what we have left behind.

I want to leave traces of truth,

traces of what it feels like,
what can be told today.

I want to read all I can,

paint all I can,

live all I can.

I HAVE TO REMEMBER THAT it's OKAY (and NORMAL + RIGHT) to not feel UP FOR it all sometimes. to feel LET DOWN BY life.

THINKING 'THIS IS IT' WHAT I'v Been STRIVING FOR But it doesn't feel like THE ANSWER — or deep peace I THOUGHT WOULD Be HERE.

deep peace deep HEART DEEP QUIET DEEP WORRY Deep KNOWING

DEEP SEA

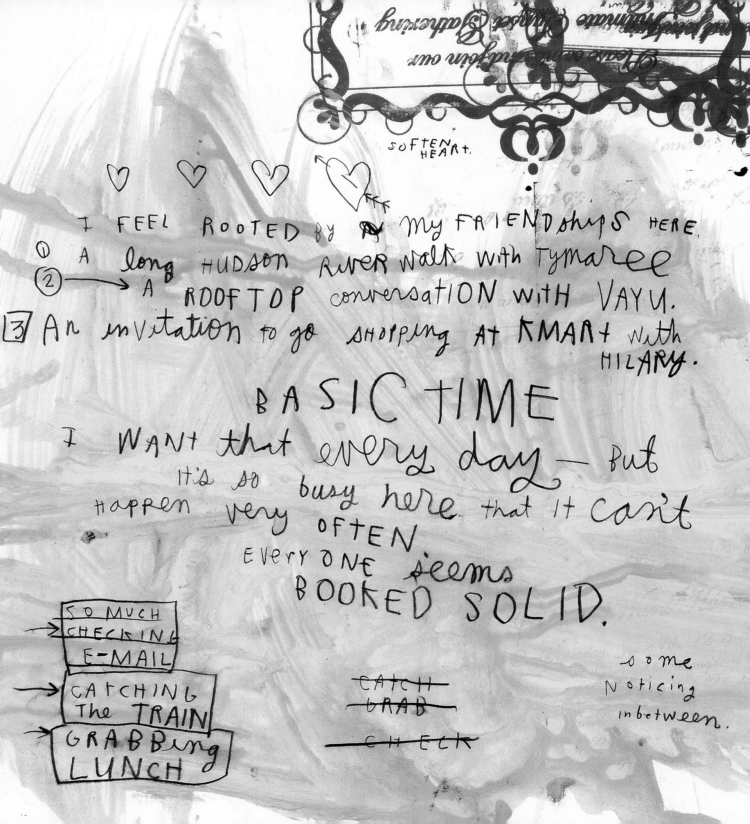

SOFTEN HEART.

I FEEL ROOTED BY MY FRIENDSHIPS HERE.

① A long HUDSON RIVER WALK with Tymaree

② → A ROOFTOP conversatION with VAYU.

③ An invitation to go shopping AT KMART with HILARY.

BASIC TIME

I WANT that every day — but It's so busy here that It can't happen very OFTEN EVERY ONE seems BOOKED SOLID.

SO MUCH CHECKING E-MAIL

CATCHING THE TRAIN

GRABBing LUNCH

~~CATCH~~
~~GRAB~~
~~CHECK~~

some Noticing inbetween.

I want a painting room.
I WANT MORNING glories
Climbing OVERhead.
I Want great mix
and backyard tAPES
wine DRINKing.
I WANt REALly LOW-KEY
FOLKS.
I WANt TO Give it UP
Give UP the COMPETITION
the city thrives ON it
THE standards are SO high
WHAT really rests at the TOP?
I don't like seeing myself in the MIRROR
trying to get there.
I look I look TRASHY when I DO.
I look BeTTER CAMPING. I feel better in P.J.'s + socks.
where can I go that is simple anyMORe?

GOOD.
BYE
NEW YORK I AM
I am saying good-bye to
Brilliant SHIFTING
Blue skies
AND SUN
shining
DOWN
Onto HARD
FLAT silver
STREETS
I am saying good-bye to cockroaches
and TINKERing
SIRENS FROM BERGEN st. Mice in the WALLS
FLATBUSH AVE → HAPPY TACO
1,9 trains A,C,E,
maybe I'll leave now so some
can return one DAY part of me
I'm off to FIND
tall grass and STARS above.
A place where
things that
I make come from in the end.

I am saying good-bye to all the places I took myself to on my PINK SEQUINED high sandals,

I am saying good-bye Gold heels flicking up as I descended the Ⓐ TRAIN to Weehawken St and Vayu's Sara around the corner roof top dream sessions CHARLES pouring Wine @ Finally Fred's Family TIES DAD's sublet apartment TYmaree adventures in the Park sleepovers at Hilary's Lloyd Miller BBQ singalongs at the E.E.E in Brooklyn

Good-BYE to the clapping for the Firefighters + rescue workers coming up the West Side Highway thank you thank you each one all along THis HAS BEEN the way HOME FOR NOW

thank you

GRANGE HALL
DOMA
Grey DOG
CORNER DISTRO

8th

168st
Ⓐ

(20 × 12 = 240)

FOllow
THe LeadeR.
WHICH leader?
why do we try to cram
all our lives into
ONe Right way?
StAND in tHe
RiGHt line?

~~Dont lose your place~~

~~strive to Fit~~

☆ ~~you~~
~~cAn~~ TAKE it OFF. you can
loosen the grip.
YOU ARE tHe Right place.

I carry WITH ME.
I carry with Me stories
OF FORGIVENESS and how
MUCH I've tried NOt to WORRY.
I carry MY worry.
I carry my concern.
I carry a green chipped painted canoe
and paddle.
I carry Dad's fishing lessons and learning
The Necessity of SILENCE, and
LOOns bobbing On the lake surface,
I carry my MOTHER's Make-up bag and
HER Wedding ring lost under the dock.
I carry with me the front steps
of every home I ever lived in—
THINKing this is it, this can be my
home from here on out.
I carry With me my hiding.
I CARRY games— 1. capture the FLAG
2. SARDINES
3. HEADS UP 7 UP
4. FOUR CORNERS

I carry with me the cheating and sneaking
AND SECRETs

SAM

I CARRY With me my pHONE and all tHE NUMBERS Of tHOSe I call and tHOSe who don't call back.

I CARRY HAIR combs for the transition hair I have going on. I carry KEYS to this sublet and keys to my storage unit in Brooklyn where all tHE OBJects I love and define ME, WAIt FOR ME TO COME get tHEM.

1. cReaky green Bed
2. cANdle sticks
3. WINE glasses
4. Pillows and old WINTER COATS
5. Boxes of Memories of tHE MOSt FAVORite DAYS
6 JeANS that are too tight.

I carry a new COLLECTION. Less notes and drawings this is filled witH MUSIC notes and wide sky guitar playing before Breakfast. Reading out loud dancing on the roof tHIS man can flip me.

the liner and powder and allergy pills and some reading for the train I carry with me a map soaked with water from a leaking water bottle FOR THE TRAPPING stinking HUMIDITY.

Now I carry with me every new fresh start,
And every final drive away
I don't carry the worry of your departure
I don't carry your number anymore or your schedule in my mind.
I carry the desire to go unnoticed and at the same time not be forgotten,
I carry the laughter.
I carry Stuart Little and
Charlotte's Web and Nancy Drew
and Pippy Longstocking
and Punky Brewster.
I carry with me those wildcats
who did it their own way.
I carry the dream of you before I knew you
and into the days to come.
I want to believe there is a bigger plan
and a I need that is above me for my life,
a way that I can trust my decisions and the way it seems to go

in LOVE

I can lose myself
Along THE ROAD.

* I want to give HIM
my care
MY TIME
if my concern
MY BODY

But I have given out,
lost the BOTTOM
of my BOAT.

* Those women who hold their own —— so STRONG
AND AND DECISIVE

They make plans BLOW me AWAY
with their girlfriends on FRIDAY + SATURDAY nights
in tHe least not concerned
FOR keeping the connection for their MAN
the LOVE,
They GO ON waltzing FORWARD
Taking CARE → STRONG CARE of themselves.
(we can love so much Better From tHis PLACE)

SHE came to dreams of
HOME with two
SHE DIDn't KNOW HOW but SHE DID it anyway
AS you go
Build. draw. journey.
MAKE. pretend.
(Believe)
ask for help.

There Really is no protection From Life.

But the Acting

Why all the protective? As if believing there is?

Careful editing and graceful completely.

The SASH of dying away to clean safety, is no clean living shield

from living

And Loving

* I don't want to be ruled by my expectations, wanting MAGIC PAINLESS Filled with LOVE + Romance PERFECT crazy love-sick Rolling and Toppling

(But you see I do)

I want him to fight FOR ME

I want a 60-cent Chinese Ruby RING, and other little sweet gifts I've never gotten jewelry OR underwear FOR GIRLS from a boy "I'm not womanly enough to be given stuff like that" voice ...if my HAIR was long... He sines that. With me But he fell in LOVE and my funny DUCK FEATHER MESS OF soft tangles.

I've noticed that I like those better that I want to be FOR.

Can't we be BOTH A → kick ass strong WOMAN and a totally DIRLY GIRL?

ALL THE WAYS WE ARE

SEPTEMBER 10.

Full THIS WAS the Last
DAY they had TOGETHER.
From Dawn till Dusk.
WAS it spent
frantic in
paying bills, FOLDING
LAUNDRY?  
Cell PHONES and
groceries?
NO Milk FOR Mac + CHeese?

THis WAS the
last full
DAY they had.

Fig. 1.

Fig. 7.

Fig. 8.

Fig. 9.

Fig. 4.

LOVE
FULL AND
ALL THE WAY

I see myself trying to imitate ~~imitate~~
your father in this picture — the picture you
took of him on the beach.

Actually, I don't really like that picture,
nor this one. They both seem posed, trying
to be coyly cute.

The more telling thing I see here is
that I'm still trying to imitate ^your father anyway.

I see I'm trying to love you that much,
knowing I can't, that I'm trying to be
that good a guy, knowing I won't.

Still, I see kindness in my eyes — why don't I
feel that way?

Sometimes I just want to slosh around in my art making. Sometimes I want to be DAINTY and classy (and lovely) for my man. Sometimes I want to never look in the mirror. And give up the show. I want to live in Spain. I want to box. I want to teach at a college and be called a professor. I want to ride horses wild in Ireland. I want to make crazy quilts. I wish this studio was quiet. I wish I wasn't so damn sensitive! I wish I was low maintenance and low-key. I wish I didn't hurt the kindest people, and I wish I was better with birthdays—and I wish I knew how to get angry.

serve serve
give give
give
listen
listen
LISTEN
make
clean
give
touch
hold
hold
hold

2

6

I HAVE lost my place in LINE.
I HAVE BEEN EXCUSED FROM THE RACE
I. Have left the group   I have fallen off THE MAIN
PATH.

Part I—The Achievement

the inspector from th
had passed since Jana
completion ng a

{ COMPROMISE }?

JOY IN THE MORNING

"No!" she screamed. "Don't!" She tried to

I LOVE YOU, I LOVE YOU, I LOVE YOU

Unconcerned with all this excitement, a Hindu pa
with dignity. He walked ve

worrie
bow abou
a treat.

CAREFUL, HE MIGHT HEAR YOU

* he tells me he can do none of it now, none of what we feel we should be able to handle.

there is so much that I don't know. and so many questions and I feel that crease in my brow

as I sit here in the half shade of 5 pm late July, a year's nearly passed.

and I think My lover

my best friend my partner, my first ever, may leave in the flash of an eye___ FOR CHINA

MOVE
+D CHINA   It seems it always could happen,

anything can take us away.

and with my fears I prepare for this loss in my heart.

The heartbreaking loneliness.

I am born with this same longing.

Dad says I am like him this way,   I _Mike Ross_

NANA ♡

* and all that is rational can tell me   it is good and right and exciting.

what are we aiming for?

choosing adventure, choosing life...choosing the road less traveled.

I think of my own life for a moment.

where do I start from here?

where do I belong?

do I head off?

to follow?

before heading out for   toothpaste   This early morning

I pause and write down again, after so long.

slowly taking note of my life while I live it

GODSEND

I know it must all be a god-sent...giving me space and my own time again, after so long.
Time to get so perspective, look at my own life with room around the edges.

some

a

American

* TODAY   MID WAY DOWN IN
           the girth Of me
           I Feel ANGRY

           And feel
           weird FOR
           NOt understanding
           WHY

ALL this NEW
relationship
Learning
AND I feel so sloppy at it.   WHAT AN
emotional MESS I feel like WADing
        THROUGH NEW
            Water.

and it all wavers

giving up on

sort of longing for a calm I thought I could hold

and know was true and right and somehow

there is a terrible sadness I feel.

a mourning of a certain sort of dream come true

lasting

THOSE
expectations
for
my work
fly away

capture the
real story

smooth down

cover over

explain

slum down

Be clear

MADE IN U.S.A.

SHORT-ORDER
COOK
RESTAURANT
CITY

15

ELEVATOR OPER.
MO.
5'4" 38
6 DAYS
ORMAN
5 FT.
REFERENCE
55 mo

PORTER-
APT-HOUSE
ROOM
MEAL
30 mo

SEA FOOD

{ the GRAND WOMAN }
DOES
prevent PREDICT PREPARE
I want us all to THROW away our lists TODAY. We Fill and fill, CHECK OFF
AND add MORE. start OVER WITH MORE TOMORROW to HOLd together
mama
show me HOW to let go

CARE TAKERS

SOMETIMES I DON'T THINK I'LL BE A GOOD MOTHER
I won't be patient AND selfless and loose
I worry how overwhelmed I will feel HOW TIRED.
I WORRY I WILL lose ME and what I MAKE.
I do know there will be nothing left to give.
deep DOWN that making another HUMAN being is the MOST creative AMAZING thing—But I still worry.
SOMETIMES I feel like I CAN'T BE A WIFE.
The fear of losing SELF FADING AWAY
nothing left for anyone else to love or need
HOW can we take CARE along the way?
RESTORE FILL UP AWAKEN
(I wanna be A good mama)

My mom seemed like she handled it all so well.
I ADMIRE the WOMEN who handle the BALANCE
I DON'T Know WHAT WE become

SCOTT'S EMULSION

Michelle said, "If I was to go back to before I had a baby, I would say —

REALLY love what you are doing NOW!
Your writing...your art.. LOVE IT!
GIVE yourself over to it NOW!
Later when you want to be a mother, you will be so glad you gave yourself this
TIME to live your work
give yourself TIME to work
HARD AT it."

off to screenprint I will go

I AM going to TRY to look up on rushing
TO TIE DOWN who I AM.
I will let it stay loose + supple
"Let myself CHANGE re-invent try it All
DIFFERENTly."

Make room
'grow pink jasmine in a room
that always
stays yours'
Remember building FORTS
AND HOW to play hard
Way PAST Dinner
REMEMBER ABOUT GRACE
AND FORGIVENESS.
Remember to let DOWN
and admit overwelm.

Subj: **Re: No Subject**
Date: Sunday, April 6, 2003 11:35:56 PM
From: Blythe
To: Sabart

yes.
thank you for coming over for tea and hasseling on the haight. what was up
with that? so nice to be and laugh with a new bad ass friend.
i must confess i listened to the rest of the ex boyfriend singing tape when
you left let's hope he wasn't visiting my upstairs neighbor.
today i thought of you when writing about shamans and medicine men for
school. they talk of the power of the "wounded healer"- the one who dares
to bare their soul, who feels the pull to do so, to guide others through the
twilight to dawn. it is the wounded healer knows the blood of the people,
and isn't afraid to show that they too are bleeding. that is their tincture,
their medicine. maybe that's what we are. maybe the medicine is in the
revealing, the baring of scraped knees and bruised hearts .
                    -blythe

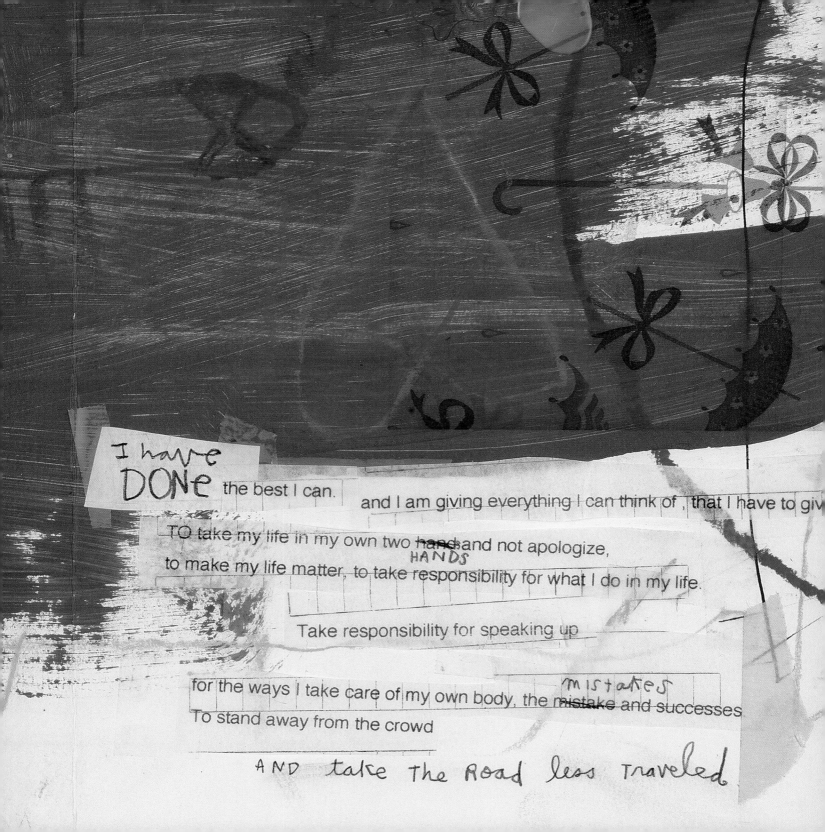

I have DONE the best I can.

and I am giving everything I can think of , that I have to giv[e]

TO take my life in my own two hand~~s~~ HANDS and not apologize,

to make my life matter, to take responsibility for what I do in my life.

Take responsibility for speaking up

for the ways I take care of my own body, the ~~mistake~~ **mistakes** and successes

To stand away from the crowd

AND take the Road less Traveled

汕头大学稿

I want to say I'm sorry for letting you down,

but I can't say sorry anymore.

Fig. 1.

I can't I just can't.

there will be no one left here.

PAON

HERE I AM, here I BEGIN.

BEGINNING OVER AND OVER
starting again with what
I KNOW NOW.

TODAY I WAKE UP FROM
a dream of a studio
A place I can make and
DANCE and
teach IN.
A place where I'm not
too BIG and
MY WORK
FITS
THE SUN COMES IN
I WANT to live just in my
STUDIO just with my colors
I DOn't want to live in the y
CONVENTIONAL WAY

I dont really WANT to live
THE WAY GROWN-UPS DO.
the way we
are trying to live
NOW- with bills
and gas and arguments
about who is going
to work on getting
CAR INSURANCE
And taking the TRASH
Out and
why does
the Bathroom smell
FUNNY??
AND WHAT ABOUT
CHANNEL 11? "Why
DONT WE GET NBC"?
and "WIll YOU TURN THAT
DOWN?"

"Honey I've got to get up early." WHEN DID IT
BECOME THIS? Why Does it have me to?
It FADES ME — DULLS ME

sometimes I just
WANT to live with sticks + Blankets
LIKE THE WAY OF THE FORT
I want to live with the moonlight
and DUSTY Backroads
I WANT to keep ON
AND TRAVEL
Light.

Monday

gran
HA

'WE MUST BE willing to GET RID OF THE *life* WE HAVE PLANNED, SO AS to HAVE THE *Life* that IS WAITING FOR US.'
~JOSEPH CAMPBELL

BARROW

Christopher st.

INVEN+ ANOTHER WAY.

I am reading RILKE'S Letters on Cézanne it's beautiful Lyrical and He writes:

"Somehow, I too must find a way of making things; not plastic, written things, but realties that arise from the craft itself. Somehow I too must discover the smallest constituent element, the cell of my art, the tangible immaterial means of expressing everything."

DAD

TODAY I WILL take GOD WITH ME
INTO my studio to sit with me slow and
HELPING ME STEADY, SOFTEN
DOWN into
JOY and MESS
TO SHOW me HOW to make something I love
tHAt FILLS ME and SPEAKS

~~feel~~

CLEAR.

Aa Bb Cc Dd Ee
Gg Hh I

*mixing colors
STREAKING
yellow WINDOW DOWN
the edge of the Rolled-out
& Brazilian
grooves
playing.
A glass of
'TWO-BUCK'
CHUCK,
IN this FLASH
of my life,
It is the
only life
I WISH
TO MAKE.
PAPER ON
the FLOOR

IN one life
HOW Many Times
CAN the HeARt
BREAK?
When DO We
KNOW We
Have FOUND OUR
TRUE NORtH?

Where DO 1 Belong?
WHAt HAPPENS
Next?

HOW DO I Know IF tHIS
IS ALL WR Ong?
HOW long Will WE
live tHIs Way?
What Will my
CHILDREN Be like?
HOW long Will I live?

WHere Will I GO?

little
RED SHOES.

Patti Griffin
U.2
Cowboy
Junkies
John
Lennon

Last Night I WAS SURROUNDED by FOLKS that I LOVE JASON, LEIGH, and JOHN. WE were all singing TOGETHER around CANDLES AND COLORED PENCILS. I soaked in the warm SONGs of My tribe.

I am filled with happiness, not PERFECT RIGHTness, just a softening of UNDERSTANDING FOR the way life is going. THIS HAS ALL happENED before US, we came from the past, from songs and FIRE and sideways glances. WE create it all over again, UNTIED and LOOSE we travel together, Making it to the Next LANDING POINt, BAGS IN FISTS, EYES WIDE OPEN

Prob. 11th Content of Land Ex. 5th
Full Solution on the opposite Page
remember to go to the sea
build
MOATS
NEW ADVENTURES
TOWERS + bridges inbetween
BAKER BEACH
I remember you

What would I be without

THANK YOU SO VERY MUCH

{I think this is the most messy thank you page possible}

thank YOU! Villard

Chris Sales

WE I love you

BRUCE Tracy Rudolph aDam Korngin annie Klein Beth

Sara Beth Cohen

BRAD Carney Kenyn Cacoin

sorry + Thank u editor

Jennifer Walsh thank you thank you thank you

Hilary Swan sweetheart love + gessy

chad Love sweethome love and family of animals

11 Weehawken street Evan

NEW YORK city

JOHN DEB KATE FAMILY

Tymaree Cook

elissa albert

Alex M. Love PHOTOGRAPHIC

Joycelyn Reid and Chris OFF TO SEA

Alexander Kopps

Vayu Ashley Kiersten

SAM Waterbury

FINALLY FRED'S & S.O.H.A.

charles chaz

LLoyd Miller E.E.E.

Sarah

the Noonan John Noonan and the love

THIS MUSIC feeds

florida city it's kinda HARD right now

FISH BOWL

KATCHIE baard MARG Jacobs YOGA

Robert RICH and Stacey

Mary and Lauren Anders

Misha Hughes FISH FARM Kim Vornado

SALEM

China

Elisabetta KATIES Lucas

Italy angel!

Shawn Justice Milo + EDWARD

SPAIN

Shantou university

Little Love

TARO

Echo Nin Nin and Fairy sweet All the students

the BBQ at the East gate.

Beautiful ART MAKER R! Robin McCloskey Christine Norton

Haley and her Horses she saves

the CORTONA workshop Ladies

Shelby JerY and Madalyn

Peggy Honeywell's music

ANDREW Paynter

AMANDA JONES Fresh air teeny grass

N.P.R.

P.R.I. P + reed

KALA

UNICEF

MISSION cultural center graphica Matei

Susi and Billy always Italy

Jill Valle fat Archer School

BOB Beauchamp and his great girls and hug Lot support

Long THE Way

Studio neighbor S. Goddess

Melanie DOHERTY

Imagine That Design Patti

Studio 212

David Hooton

The memory of Jenny

Colleen Molly

Michelle Collier Michelle Bakken

sweet soul care

Nichole Wong Read

DANCING through and Ali

Erin Hanley + ANDY!

The amazing INTERNS that became family

MUCH Michelle McAuliffe

Christine Castro

THANK YOU For making this book with me

the Berkeley PUBLIC Library

Valerie ZOE Becky Goldfisher

Suzanne Corbett Hering

MIA + CARL

Anne's Massages

Stephanie music

DOSEN BRAVE

Amy Haines in Albany Georgia and all the amazing High School students I will never forget

THANK YOU dear FOR SO MUCH CARE

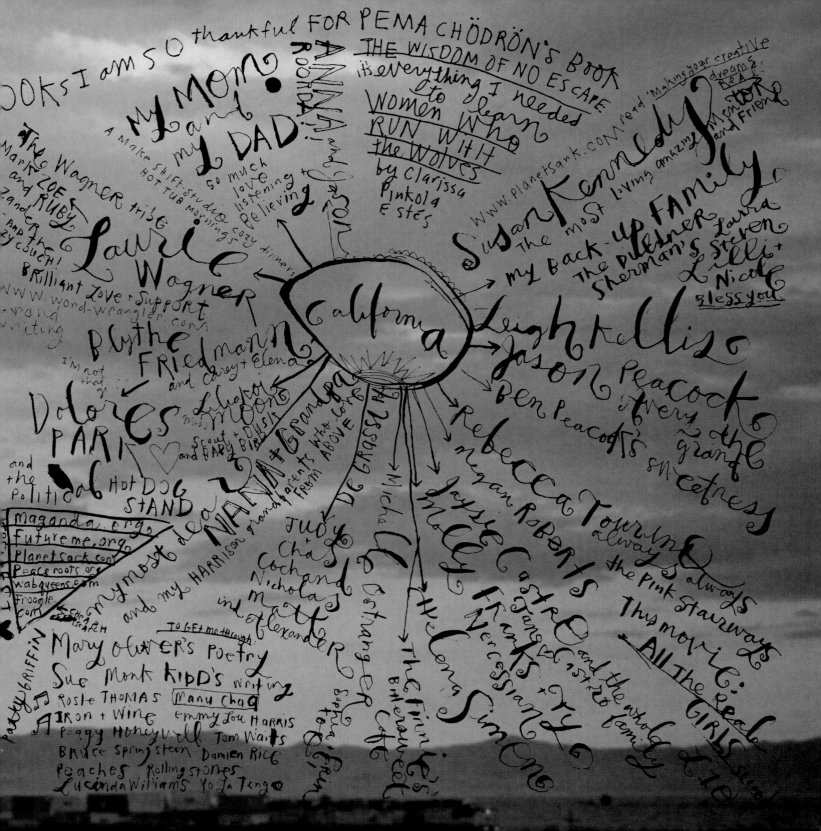

Library of Congress Cataloging-in-Publication Data

Harrison, Sabrina Ward.
   Messy thrilling life/Sabrina Ward Harrison.
      p. cm.
   ISBN 0-8129-6766-6
   1. Conduct of Life-Miscellanea. 2. Harrison, Sabrina Ward. I. Title.

BF637.C5H375 2004
158.1-dc22   2004041915

Villard Books Website address: www.villard.com
Sabrina's Website address: www.SabrinaWardharrison.com
Laurie Wagner's Website address: www.word-wrangler.com

Production interns Nichole Wong, Erin Hanley and Michelle McAuliffe
Taro Hattori production assistant for Photography   a.k.a MUCK Book production Queen.

Printed in the United States of America on acid-free paper
987654321
First Edition